Faith

Infusion

Volume Two

Faith Infusion
Volume Two

Breastplate Prayer Publications

Distributed by Frontliners Ministries
3715 Ridge Road
Charlotte, NC 28269

Cover Design: Gretta Berry
Editor: Annette Williams

All scripture is taken from the King James Version, KJV, of the Bible.
Public Domain.

Nouns and pronouns referring to deity are capitalized throughout
the text of this book unless they are included without a direct
quotation, in which case the original capitalization is retained.

Printed in the United States of America
ISBN: 978-1-7329229-9-0

Introduction

In *Faith Infusion, Volume 1*, on day 28 I identified that Apostle John didn't use the Greek word for faith, "Pistes", G4102. Faith is his entire writing! Instead, he chose to use the Greek word "Pisteuo", G4100 Believe and he used it 52 times.

The KJV translates Strong's G4100 in the following manner: believe (239x), commit unto (4x), commit to (one's) trust (1x), be committed unto (1x), be put in trust with (1x), be committed to one's trust (1x), believer (1x).

This daily 31-day infusion of Faith will not cover all 52 instances the word believe is used in the Bible but will give a coordinated selection of the word for the purpose of strengthening faith.

Believing and Faith can't really be separated from each other, at the time of salvation the Bible indicates that believing precedes faith, where believing is a heart issue and Faith is a confession issue.

Look at Romans Chapter 10 verses 9 through 11.

Romans 10:9 That if thou shalt confess with thy mouth the Lord Jesus, and shalt believe in thine heart that God hath raised him from the dead, thou shalt be saved.

Romans 10:10 For with the heart man believeth unto righteousness, and with the mouth, confession is made unto salvation.

Romans 10:11 For the scripture saith, Whosoever believeth on him shall not be ashamed.

Also in Volume 1 on day 28 the theme and colors related to each book that correspond to the colors found in the gate of the Tabernacle pitched in the wilderness are given. See Below:

Matthew = Kingship = Purple
Mark = Sacrifice = Red
Luke = Righteousness = White
John = Heavenly Origin = Blue

Notice that the gospel of John is blue for heavenly origin. Therefore the book of John is designed to get men to believe from their hearts on the one sent from heaven. John at the very beginning of his writings indicates that reality when he states "In the beginning was the Word, and the Word was with God, and the Word was God." *John 1:1*

DAY 1

Helping Men Believe

John 1:6-9; There was a man sent from God, whose name was John (the Baptist). The same came for a witness, to bear witness of the Light, that all men through him might believe. He was not that Light, but was sent to bear witness of that Light. That was the true Light, which lighteth every man that cometh into the world.

The entire assignment given by Father to John the Baptist was to get men ready for Christ.

Isaiah 40:3 The voice of him that crieth in the wilderness, Prepare ye the way of the LORD, make straight in the desert a highway for our God.

This prophetic revelation came to Isaiah long before John the Baptist was born or Jesus was dispatched from heaven. Men were being prepared by John the Baptist to accept Jesus as the Son of God. He prepared them by having them confess their faults, be baptized, and to change their hearts towards their fellow man. All done so that they could receive the Light (JESUS) and receive His blessings when He came.

People frequently claim to believe in Jesus, yet their actions belie that claim. Even those who have embraced the finished works of Jesus Christ must conduct themselves as though He has already appeared and established His heavenly kingdom on earth.

John cried out for people to repent because the heavenly kingdom was on the way.

But now we know He has come and has established His kingdom in His people. The time has come for the body of Christ to act as though heaven has descended upon the earth and given us power to proclaim the kingdom!

It is time to believe from the heart so that we can confess our faith openly to see the power of God revealed!

Notes:

_____

_____

_____

_____

_____

_____

_____

_____

_____

_____

_____

_____

_____

_____

DAY 2

Belief That Leads To Worship

John 4:19-24 The woman saith unto him, Sir, I perceive that thou art a prophet. Our fathers worshipped in this mountain; and ye say, that in Jerusalem is the place where men ought to worship. Jesus saith unto her, Woman, believe me, the hour cometh, when ye shall neither in this mountain, nor yet at Jerusalem, worship the Father.

Ye worship ye know not what: we know what we worship: for salvation is of the Jews. But the hour cometh, and now is, when the true worshippers shall worship the Father in spirit and in truth: for the Father seeketh such to worship him. God is a Spirit: and they that worship him must worship him in spirit and in truth.

Only the book of Saint John describes Jesus' interaction with the Samaritan woman. It is an amazing encounter for a host of reasons with the most obvious being that she is a Samaritan woman.

Being a Samaritan and a woman, she is startled that Jesus would even approach her. Jews and Samaritans didn't have a great relationship. Because Jews frequently encountered attacks, robberies, and even murder when they had to pass through Samaria, the two groups did not interact.

During their talk, the woman offered Jesus a great question about the ideal location of worship. She connected worship to geography and culture! Sadly, many people today still subscribe to her rationale, which holds that worship is related to their location rather than their identity.

Jesus dispels the fallacy of geography and culture and introduces an entirely new style of worship. But first, He asked that she accept the truth regarding her object of worship; He had new facts!

Jesus asked her to believe that He knew something that she didn't. This idea was related to spiritual reality rather than a physical location or culture.

Jesus is very gentle with her even though He knows everything about her. He is bringing her to the place that she can believe and enter true worship!

Remember that the person speaking to the Samaritan woman also lives inside a born-again person. So give Him your faith now and worship Him. It is your victory!

Notes:

_____

_____

_____

_____

_____

_____

_____

_____

_____

_____

_____

_____

_____

DAY 3

Experience Jesus For Yourself

John 4:42 And (The men of the city) said unto the woman, Now we believe, not because of thy saying: for we have heard him ourselves, and know that this is indeed the Christ, the Saviour of the world.

After meeting Jesus at the well, the Samaritan woman returned to the city to tell everyone about her encounter. She is the only one who has heard of this novel form of worship. Jesus also spoke to her about her past behavior and present actions. She initially questioned Him about worship because she believed He was a prophet.

Consider that this woman—whom everyone knew was promiscuous—is returning to share information about worship. She begins by letting them know that Jesus was fully aware of who she was and everything she had done before telling them what He had to say about worship.

She also informs them that He claimed to be Christ. She responds that he is a Jewish Rabbi when they question who he is. Think about the shock!

When they go to the well and ask Jesus to come to town to share His message, their emotions and hearts are deeply moved. Of course, the woman attracted their attention, so they went to the well. But thanks to Jesus' words, Father filled their hearts with faith!

It is wonderful to hear about the things of God through preaching or prophecy, but hearing Jesus for yourself is so much greater. Therefore, choose a seat and allow the Christ within you to talk about the limitless riches of the kingdom!

Develop a daily time to sit and wait on the Lord, and He will meet you at your well!

Notes:

_____

_____

_____

_____

_____

_____

_____

_____

_____

_____

_____

_____

_____

_____

DAY 4

Learn To Believe Without Evidence

John 4:46-54 So Jesus came again into Cana of Galilee, where he made the water wine. And there was a certain nobleman, whose son was sick at Capernaum. When he heard that Jesus was come out of Judaea into Galilee, he went unto him, and besought him that he would come down, and heal his son: for he was at the point of death. Then said Jesus unto him, Except ye see signs and wonders, ye will not believe. The nobleman saith unto him, Sir, come down ere my child die. Jesus saith unto him, Go thy way; thy son liveth. And the man believed the word that Jesus had spoken unto him, and he went his way.

And as he was now going down, his servants met him, and told him, saying, Thy son liveth. Then enquired he of them the hour when he began to amend. And they said unto him, Yesterday at the seventh hour the fever left him. So the father knew that it was at the same hour, in the which Jesus said unto him, Thy son liveth: and himself believed, and his whole house. This is again the second miracle that Jesus did, when he was come out of Judaea into Galilee.

The Nobleman was an authority officially working for Herod Antipas. History records that he served as Herod's steward, called Chuza. A Chuza was a prophet or seer! One of the women in Luke chapter 8 who "Ministered unto Jesus of their substance" (Luke 8:3) is this Nobleman's wife. These women, who had the resources and were prepared to share them with kingdom leaders, were referred to by Bishop Wellington Boone as the "Luke Eight Company!"

This Nobleman is here on behalf of his dying son. Jesus' earthly ministry has not yet been made evident; so far, He has transformed the water into wine. The Nobleman is requesting healing for his son based only on the basis that water turned into wine, which he must have heard about. Consider that Jesus' first recognized healing occurred in somebody from a country other than Israel.

Jesus explains to him that seeing and believing go hand in hand. As Christians, we "Believe to See," but the outside world must "See to Believe!" No matter what we see, we must approach the Lord with our hearts firmly fixed on believing in him. When an invitation to come forth for healing, blessings, etc., is offered, people frequently behave in the same way as the Nobleman.

Some people won't move until they see another person move or even until they see someone else blessed by God. We must never forget that the Lord is calling people to come forth! We must learn to act as though Jesus is there in front of people when an invitation is extended, not the person doing the ministering. Keep in mind that the invitation came from Him.

Notes:

_____

_____

_____

_____

_____

_____

_____

_____

_____

_____

_____

_____

_____

_____

DAY 5

The Works Speak

John 5:36-47 But I have greater witness than that of John: for the works which the Father hath given me to finish, the same works that I do, bear witness of me, that the Father hath sent me. And the Father himself, which hath sent me, hath borne witness of me. Ye have neither heard his voice at any time, nor seen his shape.

And ye have not his word abiding in you: for whom he hath sent, him ye believe not. Search the scriptures; for in them ye think ye have eternal life: and they are they which testify of me. And ye will not come to me, that ye might have life.

I receive not honour from men. But I know you, that ye have not the love of God in you. I am come in my Father's name, and ye receive me not: if another shall come in his own name, him ye will receive.

How can ye believe, which receive honour one of another, and seek not the honour that cometh from God only? Do not think that I will accuse you to the Father: there is one that accuseth you, even Moses, in whom ye trust.

For had ye believed Moses, ye would have believed me: for he wrote of me. But if ye believe not his writings, how shall ye believe my words?

It isn't easy to start writing on these verses because there is so much content. I don't want to write a book within a book as these faith infusions are designed to be short. I will thus begin where Jesus says Moses wrote about Him at the conclusion. And he did! Review the list below.

> The Passover Lamb
> The Desert Manna
> Water from the Rock
> The Wilderness Serpent lifted
> The Lion of Judah
> Benjamin, Son of my right hand
> Isaac, the One and Only Son, Offered as the Sacrifice
> Jacob's hands crossed over Joseph's two sons
> The Son of the Woman Who Crushes the Head of the Snake

All are references to Jesus!

People's failure to abide in God's word is the problem Jesus is addressing! You have to realize that most people in this period couldn't read. They, therefore, proceeded to the synagogue to hear the Torah read by the Jewish elders. Jesus explains to them that although they have heard the Bible, living it and believing it are two very different things.

Join me in thinking for a moment! We believe the Father sent Jesus to earth to save the lost and undo the devil's schemes. Men received inspiration from Father God to write about His earthly activities! Holy Spirit is a guide who Jesus sent to help us understand the truth of the Bible and apply it to our lives.

We aren't making progress, though, having confidence in Jesus' name. The challenges we confront seem to have more influence and control over us than God's word does! Less than 20% of Christ's body reads the Bible every day. These Infusions are made to help you stay on task each day so that you may start to notice changes in your life. Is it working?

More faith will be developed in the Lord through Bible study than even listening to preaching. So put the word at the forefront of your life and take pleasure in the fruits of your growing faith! Without neglecting the preached word!

Notes:

_____

_____

_____

_____

_____

_____

_____

_____

_____

_____

_____

_____

_____

DAY 6

The Only Work Needed

John 6:29-30 Jesus answered and said unto them, This is the work of God, that ye believe on him whom he hath sent. They said therefore unto him, What sign shewest thou then, that we may see, and believe thee? what dost thou work?

John 6:36 But I said unto you, That ye also have seen me, and believe not.

John 6:64 But there are some of you that believe not. For Jesus knew from the beginning who they were that believed not, and who should betray him.

John 6:69 And we believe and are sure that thou art that Christ, the Son of the living God.

One of the most explosive chapters in the Bible is Saint John, chapter six. Our focus will be the five verses in which the word "believe" appears. The people's first question was how to carry out Jesus' works.

While responding to their questions, Jesus utilized it to address future generations. Believing in Jesus, whom the Father sent to Earth to advance His kingdom, is the only effort necessary. Many attending church services regularly and even some reading this book would claim to have believed, but have they?

One day, as I was waiting in a very long line, it dawned on me that God had come to Earth in the person of Jesus Christ. AS A MAN, HE DID SO! Every day the Lord stepped on the Earth, it celebrated! The very ground was supporting the Creator that called it into existence.

That day, faith erupted in my heart! All I had to do was trust that Jesus had been sent and had arrived to finish the task given! Amen!

Some people standing listening to Jesus and asking the question refused to believe that God sent him even though they had witnessed His miracles and heard His messages, which far surpassed those of the religious leaders of their time! Jesus knew that Judas was one of the unbelievers even though he was a chosen disciple.

In an instant, Jesus took those listening up into spiritual attitudes that they weren't ready for. He told them they had to eat His flesh and drink His blood to grow spiritually! Most left and never walked with Jesus again after He told them they had to consume His flesh and blood. Remember, their question was that they wanted additional information or signs to believe He was the one!

He then questioned the disciples, asking if they would also depart.

They have nowhere to go; according to Peter, they had the conviction that Jesus was the Christ, the Son of the Living God!

Think for a moment, how committed are you in believing that Jesus was sent to earth by the Father and nothing or no one can change your mind!

Notes:

_____

_____

_____

_____

_____

_____

_____

_____

_____

_____

_____

_____

_____

_____

DAY 7

Family Unbelief Stops Nothing

John 7:5 For neither did his brethren believe in him.

It can be challenging to convince your family to support you sometimes. Take comfort in the knowledge that Jesus' family also struggled to understand what He was doing when these situations crop up in your life, especially when it comes to serving the Father and His Kingdom.

We know Mary knew who He was and the circumstances surrounding His entry into the world. And now that Joseph is deceased, she is the only person who truly knows. She had undoubtedly told them the tale, but the knowledge seemed too much for them to comprehend, so they made their own judgments.

Jesus refused to let the disbelief of his brother alter His course or goal. And you cannot either! Keep going; you never know how Father will use you to reach your family. Remember that James, who becomes a leader in the body of believers, is Jesus' brother. The book of James nevertheless addresses spiritual subjects in ways that Jesus did not. History demonstrates that the entire family follows the person they used to call brother but changes to Lord, and He brings them into the kingdom's reality!

Never let others alter what your Father has instructed you to do. Counseling by mature leaders is always essential because we tend to move too fast, but keep moving! It's time for you to claim more territory for heaven!

Notes:

_____

_____

_____

_____

_____

_____

_____

_____

_____

_____

_____

_____

_____

_____

DAY 8

Your Belief Produces Rivers Of Living Water

John 7:37-39 In the last day, that great day of the feast, Jesus stood and cried, saying, If any man thirst, let him come unto me, and drink. He that believeth on me, as the scripture hath said, out of his belly shall flow rivers of living water. (But this spake he of the Spirit, which they that believe on him should receive: for the Holy Ghost was not yet given; because that Jesus was not yet glorified.)

The seven-day Sukkot (Tabernacles) holiday is the festival mentioned in John Chapter 7. The following day is "Shemini Atzeret," the eight-day, a special holy day associated with the Sukkot festival.

Although it's unclear whether Jesus made this proclamation on the seventh or eighth day of the festival, I'm willing to bet he did on the eighth. Many think that since the Tabernacle was the last feast, the eighth day will begin when Jesus returns and that we must wait for those days.

I can see their point of view, but I still believe that Jesus' death, burial, and resurrection signaled the beginning of a brand-new era. You can read about creation in the book of Genesis, and you'll see that each day concludes with the phrase "The Evening and The Morning." The only day this didn't take place was the seventh day, which God blessed and instructed man to observe as a holy day of rest. I think Jesus said, "It Is Finished," on the cross to signal the end of the seventh day. His cry was the "Evening and Morning" proclamation that the seventh day didn't receive in the beginning!

He also announced a new day, kingdom, way to be born, and power that would manifest in three days. Keep this in mind while reading the following verse from Psalm 118.

Psalm 118:24 This is the day which the LORD hath made; we will rejoice and be glad in it.

It's not referring to a specific day in time; instead, It's referring to a brand-new day that all other days abide in—a day connected to the other seven but stands alone. The fact that every name and title connected to Jesus through the Greek language is a multiple of eight is one of the ways I arrived at this conclusion. Jesus is a brand-new beginning.

The name Jesus (Ιησούς) in Greek has a numerical value of 888! Learn more about all of Jesus' names, titles, and numerical values in my book *Knowing God By The Numbers*. You can find this book at https://www.BishopLarryJackson.com.

I think it was on "Shemini Atzeret" for a second reason: the promise. Rivers of Living Water would flow out of those who believe in Him. In this passage, Jesus refers to the Holy Spirit, which humans will receive eight days following his resurrection. The qualifications were to thirst for JESUS and trust in him!

There were two Sabbaths during the Feast of Tabernacles. On the first day, one, and on the eighth day, the other! The author of Hebrews asserts that a New Rest is available to those in Christ in contrast to the rest of the old covenant. Christ-followers enjoy constant, 24/7 rest that isn't based on laws and regulations but rather on the power of the spirit!

The time has come for the body to access all eighth-day advantages through the Holy Spirit.

Notes:

_____

_____

_____

_____

_____

_____

_____

_____

_____

_____

_____

_____

_____

_____

DAY 9

Embrace The Truth And Believe

John 8:21-24 Then said Jesus again unto them, I go my way, and ye shall seek me, and shall die in your sins: whither I go, ye cannot come. Then said the Jews, Will he kill himself? because he saith, Whither I go, ye cannot come. And he said unto them, Ye are from beneath; I am from above: ye are of this world; I am not of this world. I said therefore unto you, that ye shall die in your sins: for if ye believe not that I am he, ye shall die in your sins.

John 8:45-46 And because I tell you the truth, ye believe me not. Which of you convinceth me of sin? And if I say the truth, why do ye not believe me?

Jesus is speaking to the temple's religious authorities, not the general public, out on the streets. He is battling their refusal to accept what they ought to know already. These are the individuals who research and discuss the Old Testament manuscripts. These are the people whose hearts are open to the Messiah but who regrettably want Him to arrive in accordance with their plans.

They find it challenging to comprehend a Kingdom entirely different from what they had anticipated. Even though they stand for divine truth to the people, truth is not resonating in their hearts. According to the Bible, their inability to hear or see was caused by their hearts being too rigid.

We must always check our hearts and ask ourselves tough questions about why we resist or defend issues. Sometimes simple things can cause us to miss JESUS when He is there to help! These well-trained religious leaders did, and so can we.

Notes:

_____

_____

_____

_____

_____

_____

_____

_____

_____

_____

_____

_____

_____

_____

DAY 10

Only Believe And Nothing Is Impossible

John 9:18 But the Jews did not believe concerning him, that he had been blind, and received his sight, until they called the parents of him that had received his sight.

John 9:35-38 Jesus heard that they had cast him out; and when he had found him, he said unto him, Dost thou believe on the Son of God? He answered and said, Who is he, Lord, that I might believe on him? And Jesus said unto him, Thou hast both seen him, and it is he that talketh with thee. And he said, Lord, I believe. And he worshipped him.

I love this miracle and all the difficulties it caused the religious leaders. Nobody had ever witnessed an individual who was born blind regain their sight. When the disciples realized that the guy was born blind, they inquired as to whether his blindness resulted from his fault or the wrongdoing of his parents.

Remembering that the previous covenant said a parent's sin could pass on to four generations. So

.

that seemed a reasonable question to ask. They certainly seemed astonished by Jesus' response.

We must realize that while sin did make him blind, Adam's sin did it. Death came to Earth through Adam, bringing disease, sickness, and all kinds of infirmities. Consequently, his parents were not directly responsible for his blindness!

Jesus declares that the blindness would bring glory to Father! There was a huge uproar when the blind beggar that everyone knew received healing. The man is thrilled and enthusiastic as he explains that he can see.

The Jewish authorities intended to act as though they were unaware of the man's existence and had not seen the same blind man for many years. They demanded extra proof from his parents that he was born blind rather than accepting the miracle!

His parents confirmed that he was their Son and had been born blind, but they didn't know how he got his sight. No matter what Jesus did, these leaders refused to accept Him!

Even though the man questioned them and argued that Jesus could not be a sinner because He had opened His eyes, they expelled him. Everyone was aware that God does not hear sinners. He genuinely has no idea who Jesus was or where He went, though! He knows that although he was once blind, he can now see.

Jesus once again proves that He is the Son of God in this situation! He asks the man if he believes when He comes across him after being kicked out of the synagogue. The man not only had faith, but he also worshipped Jesus!

It is time for us to intensify our worship if we know Jesus is Lord.

Notes:

DAY 11

Sheep Believe The Shepherd

John 10:26 But ye believe not, because ye are not of my sheep, as I said unto you.
John 10:37-38 If I do not the works of my Father, believe me not. But if I do, though ye believe not me, believe the works: that ye may know, and believe, that the Father is in me, and I in him.

This chapter is crucial for the modern assembly. The chapter opens with Jesus giving a parable about two sheep owners and their sheep (us). One is the theft, robbers, and thugs (religious leaders) who steal the sheep from their valid owner or the actual Shepherd (Jesus). He is the lawful owner who cares for the flock and is willing to give His life for them.

If you read the chapter, you will see that we have been misusing verse 10 for many years. Most churchgoers misinterpret Jesus' teaching by focusing on the Devil when they quote the verse. He was referring to religious authorities who believed they owned the sheep and had stolen their skills, put an end to their goals, and took away their motivation to serve GOD!

And this is still happening in the Christian world today. The thieves and robbers are overlooked because our attention is on the Devil, who Jesus overcame and destroyed his handiwork.

Jesus continues to deal with these people even to the chapter's conclusion. Because after having witnessed His works, they choose not to believe. They have been waiting for God to appear, but they won't believe when he does because they want it the way they have determined.

Why?

Religious leaders desire to be praised and honored by the sheep!

Religious leaders are not owners; simply stewards! In the name of Jesus, make sure the leaders you are following point you toward Jesus and not themselves!

Notes:

_____

_____

_____

_____

_____

_____

_____

_____

_____

_____

_____

_____

_____

_____

DAY 12

Next World Evidence

John 11:15 And I am glad for your sakes that I was not there, to the intent ye may believe; nevertheless let us go unto him.
John 11:25-27 Jesus said unto her, I am the resurrection, and the life: he that believeth in me, though he were dead, yet shall he live: And whosoever liveth and believeth in me shall never die. Believest thou this? She saith unto him, Yea, Lord: I believe that thou art the Christ, the Son of God, which should come into the world.

We realize Jesus was aware of Lazarus' illness before the message arrived and knew how to prevent Lazarus' death; we learn crucial information about His prayer practice.

Jesus was constantly working to prepare the disciples for the day they would be in charge of the church.

No one had ever witnessed or heard about the miracle Jesus was about to perform. After being dead for four days, a person returns to life. Jesus waited before going to Lazarus' tomb to increase the disciples' faith.

When He finally showed up, Martha rushed outside to greet Him and ask Him why He hadn't shown up when she sent the message. Mary was undoubtedly processing her emotions and didn't even bother walking out to meet Him. Jesus frequented their home, and they fed Him and offered Him food. But when they most needed him, he was absent.

It's clear that He postponed His visit so the sisters could cope with their core convictions. We often want the Lord to help us instantly when we encounter issues and pray about them. If nothing happens, feelings we usually keep hidden from ourselves come to the surface. What do you do with those thoughts is the question.

We must adopt an attitude of "even if He doesn't," resolving to never mistrust the Father. By serving as a constant reminder that serving God is about serving Him, not about serving what He has done for us. He has already bestowed upon us salvation, the greatest blessing! When Martha arrived, she admitted that she thought Jesus was the Christ, the Son of God, and the conqueror of the world.

It was now time for LAZARUS to awaken from his four-day slumber covered with grave cloths laid in a grave! Nothing in our lives is so lifeless that Jesus can't bring it to life and make it work the way He wants it to! Can I get an amen?

Notes:

_____

_____

_____

_____

_____

_____

_____

_____

_____

_____

_____

_____

_____

_____

DAY 13

Glory Of God Seen Through Believing

John 11:40 Jesus saith unto her, Said I not unto thee, that, if thou wouldest believe, thou shouldest see the glory of God?
John 11:42 And I knew that thou hearest me always: but because of the people which stand by I said it, that they may believe that thou hast sent me.
John 11:48 If we let him thus alone, all men will believe on him: and the Romans shall come and take away both our place and nation.

Jesus' ability to revive Lazarus from the dead gave his disciples additional assurance while also grabbing the attention of the religious leaders. No one has ever seen or heard of a person rising from the dead after four days, as I said on Day 12.

Naturally, word of the miracle quickly traveled, and many people made long trips to see the man raised from the dead. However, Jesus' primary goal was to demonstrate the majesty of God to His disciples and sisters of Lazarus.

The religious leaders devised a plan to kill Jesus and Lazarus. Because Jesus accomplished a stunning miracle that might catch Rome's attention, Lazarus would serve as a living reminder of the event and Jesus.

They did all these things because they thought people would turn their allegiance, honor, and attention to Christ.

We should apply Some of this story's critical components to real life!

It is essential to deal with the stone of the tomb first. Usually, you need help from someone else to move your stone. To start the journey of emancipation, you need a spiritual leader who has the power to give the proper instructions and commands.

Second, the spiritual leader must think that all they do is done for the glory of God, not for their benefit.

Third, although the stone represents death, once it is removed, the possibility of life is shown. Remember that a stone had to shift for Jesus to be raised from the dead and granted access to eternal life.

Deliverance must still occur more violently, even after removal of the stone; the individual's release from whatever is holding them!

So, spiritual leaders must praise God before reaching their goal to show that everything they do is for God.

Fifth, the first three instructions are "Come Forth, Loose Them, and Let Them Go!" Leave the place that has been keeping you for all these days that symbolizes death. Nobody believes you can be free since they've held you for so long. "But God,"

Sixth, take off the burial robes! They still have restrictions while being alive and free from the grave. Many of the participants in this scenario have been awakened from the dead but are still wearing tomb clothing.

Seventh, "Go" into the very destiny God has planned. This symbolizes God's ability to perform miracles after removing the grave coverings. At this time, use your spiritual authority to release those in need from their coffin-bound state and call them out!

Notes:

_____

_____

_____

_____

_____

_____

_____

_____

_____

_____

_____

_____

_____

DAY 14

Believe In The WORD!

John 14:1 Let not your heart be troubled: ye believe in God, believe also in me.

We divide the Godhead into three distinct personalities and attempt to comprehend them from that perspective. There is only one true God, the Lord! Listen to how we say things: Jesus is God's Word, God's Spirit, God is with us in Immanuel, and so on.

Jesus says the same thing: trust in me as you do God, and your problems will disappear!

Have you ever thought that the Bible is the inspired word of God? Jesus, in your hands! Do you believe what you read? Are you seeking further assurance?

God has just spoken; thus, there's no need for additional confirmation! When reading the Bible, always have a pen and paper handy to write down the Rhema of the text.

Notes:

_____

_____

_____

_____

_____

_____

_____

_____

_____

_____

_____

_____

_____

_____

DAY 15

The Works Still Speak

John 14:11 Believe me that I am in the Father, and the Father in me: or else believe me for the very works' sake.

Jesus gives the disciples, religious leaders, and people following Him two options. Come to the place where you believe that I am the incarnation of the Father on earth or believe based on the fact I have done things no one on earth has ever done!

> Raise a dead man after four days
> Heal a blind man who was blind from birth
> Feed a multitude of people with a small lunch
> Walk on water
> Heal a woman who only touches my clothes
> Change water into wine

These are just a few fantastic miracles they clearly knew He had performed. Check John's testimony at the end of the gospel.

John 21:25 And there are also many other things which Jesus did, the which, if they should be written every one, I suppose that even the world itself could not contain the books that should be written. Amen.

But Jesus asked them to believe from a more excellent place than the miracles performed. He wanted them to believe that the God of the universe was standing before them and believe that from their hearts!

Tell me, why do you believe? Have you come to a place where nothing else is necessary because your heart is settled that God came to the planet and salvation came through Him? You received that salvation; therefore, you are now a citizen of heaven. No other miracle is needed because your life change is the greatest and most notable miracle you need!

Can someone say, Thank You JESUS?

Notes:

_____

_____

_____

_____

_____

_____

_____

_____

_____

_____

_____

_____

_____

DAY 16

Prophesy That You Believe

John 14:26-30 But the Comforter, which is the Holy Ghost, whom the Father will send in my name, he shall teach you all things, and bring all things to your remembrance, whatsoever I have said unto you. Peace I leave with you, my peace I give unto you: not as the world giveth, give I unto you. Let not your heart be troubled, neither let it be afraid. Ye have heard how I said unto you, I go away, and come again unto you. If ye loved me, ye would rejoice, because I said, I go unto the Father: for my Father is greater than I.

And now I have told you before it come to pass, that, when it is come to pass, ye might believe. Hereafter I will not talk much with you: for the prince of this world cometh, and hath nothing in me. But that the world may know that I love the Father; and as the Father gave me commandment, even so I do. Arise, let us go hence.

Jesus is once more preparing his followers for what is to come. We also recognize that one of the primary duties of the Holy Spirit is to instruct and remind people of all Jesus told them and demonstrated to them. Jesus reminds them again not to let their hearts be overtaken by trouble since He knew it was just around the corner.

Jesus assures them that although He would depart and go to the Father, He would also return. They're not paying attention and might have assumed it was another story. Even though it wouldn't look good for him, Jesus was securing their hearts and minds to believe, even though it seemed like everything was lost.

Their trust ought to have been unwavering based on what they knew and had witnessed. They should have prepared for something magnificent to happen throughout Jesus' death, burial, and resurrection. Especially Peter, James, and John because they were on the mountain of transfiguration. They also witnessed a man having his ear amputated and then naturally placed back on his head.

What do you believe many members of the body of Christ would do if the person they thought could free them from oppression was taken, placed in prison, beaten, and slain in their presence? Would they flee and hide or stay put and hold fast? The simple solution is to look at what has happened due to our day's problems. Are we standing or hiding!?

Ephesians 6:13-14 Wherefore take unto you the whole armour of God, that ye may be able to withstand in the evil day, and having done all, to

stand. Stand therefore, having your loins girt about with truth, and having on the breastplate of righteousness;

Keeping Standing!

Notes:

_____

_____

_____

_____

_____

_____

_____

_____

_____

_____

_____

_____

_____

DAY 17

Are You Sure You Believe?

John 16:30-31 Now are we sure that thou knowest all things, and needest not that any man should ask thee: by this we believe that thou camest forth from God. Jesus answered them, Do ye now believe?

The disciples still claim to think that Jesus is the one who sprang from God after all this time!

Can you see them exchanging glances as a sign of satisfaction and confirmation that they have reached their destination? How many times had Jesus emphasized this critical point to them? When they were at Caesarea Philippi, Peter understood that He was the Christ, Son of the Living God!

Jesus interrupted their revelry by asking them another question.

Do you now believe this?

He warns them that they will flee from Him and abandon Him when He most needs them. They cut ties with the Lord when the problems began and returned to their houses. Consider the mercy God showed these men despite their doubt and rejection of Jesus!

We occasionally let Jesus down in our lives and even reject Him. He does everything necessary to remove the impediments from our lives, however, and returns us to the path we were on.

The grace of God is still astounding! And we need it daily! Amen!

Notes:

_____

_____

_____

_____

_____

_____

_____

_____

_____

_____

_____

_____

_____

DAY 18

Believing Without Seeing Anything

John 17:20-21 Neither pray I for these alone, but for them also which shall believe on me through their word; That they all may be one; as thou, Father, art in me, and I in thee, that they also may be one in us: that the world may believe that thou hast sent me.

Through the disciples' writings, Jesus includes those of us who have embraced Him in the high priestly prayer of Saint John 17. As a result, we are entitled to everything He prayed for the disciples and apostles.

It feels like Jesus is speaking directly to us! Is it not astounding that His words transcend from His day to ours? Jesus is pleading that we all work together as one body, just as God is one.

While the question of whether Jesus was God manifest in the flesh remains a topic of debate, the potential impact of the body of Christ functioning in divine unity is undeniable. Such unity could provide profound answers and insights, transcending mere facts and leading to a deeper understanding.

The apostle Luke wrote of this oneness in the Book of Acts, using the Greek homothymadon, which means complete agreement. He used the word twelve times only in the Book of Acts. I think he intended to make people who would eventually come to Christianity realize how vital one accord was.

The unity of the first-century believers was a significant factor in their influence! As everyone in Rome realized, they were a formidable force because of their solidarity and kingdom mentality.
Please pray that revelation, not adversity, will bring the body of Christ back to the location of divine oneness! Make the connection with kingdom-minded believers first, and every joint will supply!

Ephesians 4:16 From whom the whole body fitly joined together and compacted by that which every joint supplieth, according to the effectual working in the measure of every part, maketh increase of the body unto the edifying of itself in love.

Notes:

_____

_____

_____

_____

_____

_____

_____

_____

_____

_____

_____

_____

_____

DAY 19

Doubt Is A True Enemy

John 20:25 The other disciples therefore said unto him, We have seen the Lord. But he said unto them, Except I shall see in his hands the print of the nails, and put my finger into the print of the nails, and thrust my hand into his side, I will not believe.

Have you ever come across someone doubtful? They have the power to frustrate you greatly! This person typically needs to believe what is spoken, but their stubbornness and unbelief prevent them from doing so.

Thomas says that until he could touch the wounds of Jesus, he would not believe.

He remained unconvinced despite hearing from reliable sources that they had firsthand knowledge.

How are you going to handle this person? You will do nothing, just like the disciples and apostles did! However, you can pray that Jesus will make himself or the things required for belief apparent to the person. Then you continue to minister and carry out your duties from the place you know to be true while you wait on the Lord to make Himself or what is required clear!

John 20:26-29 And after eight days again his disciples were within, and Thomas with them: then came Jesus, the doors being shut, and stood in the midst, and said, Peace be unto you.

Then saith he to Thomas, Reach hither thy finger, and behold my hands; and reach hither thy hand, and thrust it into my side: and be not faithless, but believing. And Thomas answered and said unto him, My Lord and my God. Jesus saith unto him, Thomas, because thou hast seen me, thou hast believed: blessed are they that have not seen, and yet have believed.

Jesus mentions us once again as those who will believe even though we have never seen Him while He was on earth. I believe that in heaven, our faith is slightly more weighted than that of those who saw Him! Stay faithful, Body of Christ!

Notes:

DAY 20

Helping The Belief Of Those Who Read

John 20:30-31 And many other signs truly did Jesus in the presence of his disciples, which are not written in this book: But these are written, that ye might believe that Jesus is the Christ, the Son of God; and that believing ye might have life through his name.

John 21:25 And there are also many other things which Jesus did, the which, if they should be written every one, I suppose that even the world itself could not contain the books that should be written. Amen.

If they recorded everything Jesus accomplished, there wouldn't be sufficient room on the entire planet! Men frequently claim that actions taken that they haven't read about in the Bible are extra-biblical. But that doesn't imply He didn't do it because it wasn't written! Their purpose in writing was to strengthen our faith, not to record every moment of Jesus' life.

I'm not saying this to make us odd; instead, I'm saying this to keep our minds open to whatever the Father wants us to do. By the way, He continues to work miracles daily through people who trust in Him!

Chapter twenty is the last time belief is mentioned in the book of John, but I still encourage you to read it again and let your faith grow. Read a chapter every day for 21 days, and you'll see remarkable growth in your faith!

Notes:

DAY 21

Lame Man Now Walking

Faith is used 15 Times in the Book of Acts

Act 3:11-16; And as the lame man which was healed held Peter and John, all the people ran together unto them in the porch that is called Solomon's, greatly wondering. And when Peter saw it, he answered unto the people, Ye men of Israel, why marvel ye at this? or why look ye so earnestly on us, as though by our own power or holiness we had made this man to walk? The God of Abraham, and of Isaac, and of Jacob, the God of our fathers, hath glorified his Son Jesus; whom ye delivered up, and denied him in the presence of Pilate, when he was determined to let him go. But ye denied the Holy One and the Just, and desired a murderer to be granted unto you; And killed the Prince of life, whom God hath raised from the dead; whereof we are witnesses. And his name through faith in his name hath made this man strong, whom ye see and know: yea, the faith which is by him hath given him this perfect soundness in the presence of you all.

As the Lord had promised, the Holy Ghost has come, and His power has been given to the faithful disciples. This same Peter, who three times denied

Jesus because he was afraid for his life, now has a newfound fearlessness.

When someone says they are ready to pray or have concluded their prayers, the lame guy sits in a lovely position outside the temple door and begs for alms. The man in question has positioned himself strategically in front of the temple. So many people have spotted him there and given him money.

This day is unique because it's the first time men filled with the Holy Spirit would see him who now has Jesus' compassion. When Peter and John told the stranger to look at them, he must have had high expectations, but they immediately dispelled any such hopes by telling him they were penniless.

They tell him that they have something better. The man needs substantial money to suit his necessities, although healing is preferable. They took hold of him and instructed for healing to occur, which it did!

Everyone now regards Peter and John as exceptional individuals with remarkable skills! Many men would let themselves believe that and claim the Lord's glory for themselves!

Seeking an explanation, these guys explained to others that their faith in Jesus caused the man's movement and standing. As a result, they have complete authority in Jesus' name, and the body of

Christ uses signs and miracles to carry out His name and advance the kingdom.

Although the body of Christ has used the name in worship, it is now time to carry it into the marketplace so that those who do not know Jesus can experience Jesus' miracle-working power! Note that neither Peter nor John used force to enter; God unlocked the door! Tell the Father you are willing to be a living example of Christ's authority and watch as He opens doors for you!

Notes:

DAY 22

7 Men Of Faith

Acts 6:5 And the saying pleased the whole multitude: and they chose Stephen, a man full of faith and of the Holy Ghost, and Philip, and Prochorus, and Nicanor, and Timon, and Parmenas, and Nicolas a proselyte of Antioch:
Acts 6:7 And the word of God increased; and the number of the disciples multiplied in Jerusalem greatly; and a great company of the priests were obedient to the faith.
Acts 6:8 And Stephen, full of faith and power, did great wonders and miracles among the people.

Observe that the persons selected to be Deacons are men of great faith. Thus, while the Deacons in the church I grew up in were decent men, I wouldn't characterize them as men of great faith. Furthermore, none of them performed extraordinary miracles or wonders among the people. Would we be chosen among our peers to serve them unto the Lord?

The Apostles promised they would neither wait on tables nor provide this kind of service to people. Instead, they committed themselves to prayer and the Word of God. Many people today may become irate and even quit their churches if the Pastor doesn't assist them on a Deacon's level.

WHY?

The Deacons' office hasn't been supported as the ones who should help the organization and spread the news to the membership!

The entire body of Christ should think and act like Deacons in their local communities. When others inquire about Jesus, be prepared to respond and show your confidence in HIM by doing signs and wonders. Then, as more and more people come to know our Lord, observe how the body of Christ grows!

Notes:

_____

_____

_____

_____

_____

_____

_____

_____

_____

_____

_____

_____

_____

_____

DAY 23

Cripple From Birth Healed

Acts 14:8-10 And there sat a certain man at Lystra, impotent in his feet, being a cripple from his mother's womb, who never had walked: The same heard Paul speak: who stedfastly beholding him, and perceiving that he had faith to be healed, Said with a loud voice, Stand upright on thy feet. And he leaped and walked.

The entry of the word of God brings light! In this instance, the light strengthened the man's faith to the point where he thought he could walk despite never having done so. The lame man, Barnabas, and Paul did not have a conversation, according to the scriptures. Instead, Paul saw the man's spirit of faith and realized that the man's healing was possible.

Everything may change when faith is present, regardless of what it is, how long it has been in a person's life, or who did it. The purpose of preaching and teaching the word of God is to help listeners develop a stronger faith. **Romans 10:17 So then faith cometh by hearing, and hearing by the word of God.**

To strengthen your faith, ask the Lord to speak to your heart during worship services where the word is being spoken or taught. As you read the Daily Infusion of Faith, pray for revelation and understanding to strengthen your faith. Act on what has been revealed immediately, and seek the Lord while He is still available! (Isaiah 55:6)

This man was born lame! He was carried around since the day he came onto the earth and undoubtedly learned to drag himself or had something made for him to roll around. Now, he is standing and moving around freely because of the word's entry!

The observers are so touched that they believe Barnabas and Paul to be gods! Paul immediately shifts the focus away from them and puts it on Jesus! Consider the attitude of the donkey Jesus rode into the city; the donkey realized the hosannas weren't for him. In like fashion, Paul and Barnabas understood it wasn't their ability or greatness that healed the man!

Jesus will enable even more of His power to operate in our lives when we put Him first! So that others can see God!

Notes:

_____

_____

_____

_____

_____

_____

_____

_____

_____

_____

_____

_____

_____

DAY 24

Left For Dead, But God!

Acts 14:19-23 And there came thither certain Jews from Antioch and Iconium, who persuaded the people, and, having stoned Paul, drew him out of the city, supposing he had been dead. Howbeit, as the disciples stood round about him, he rose up, and came into the city: and the next day he departed with Barnabas to Derbe.

And when they had preached the gospel to that city, and had taught many, they returned again to Lystra, and to Iconium, and Antioch, Confirming the souls of the disciples, and exhorting them to continue in the faith, and that we must through much tribulation enter into the kingdom of God. And when they had ordained them elders in every church, and had prayed with fasting, they commended them to the Lord, on whom they believed.

They thought the apostle Paul was dead due to the stoning outside of town. When declaring that life will go on until God determines it is over, this is one location we might cite. But keep in mind that Paul lived for and by God's will! Paul could have died that way, but it wouldn't have brought glory to Father, which is why I believe God raised him to life.

Father restored life to his body while the disciples saw; it should be no surprise that he was also healed. The very next day, he returned to his task of sharing the gospel with the believers. After this seemingly miraculous miracle, their faith undoubtedly deepened, and Paul was there to help them do so.

We must accept that nothing can stop us until God fulfills our mission! Mental exhaustion creeps in, and we may give in to the issues when life becomes challenging or we cannot see clearly. Remember that Jesus has conquered the world, and ensure you are serving God according to His will! Hold fast to your faith and see how God works for you!

Notes:

_____

_____

_____

_____

_____

_____

_____

_____

_____

_____

_____

_____

_____

_____

DAY 25

The Gentiles Saved

Acts 14:27 And when they were come, and had gathered the church together, they rehearsed all that God had done with them, and how he had opened the door of faith unto the Gentiles.

Rehearsing the victories we experience in God for our souls and a method to strengthen the confidence of other believers is a fundamental principle that is sometimes forgotten in the body of Christ today.

The church testimony service of the past was set at the beginning of the service so people could talk about what God had done in their lives.

To get attention, people started repeating the same things throughout testimony services, making them more religious. The service had shifted from being about Jesus to being about the people.

Traditional testimony sessions can potentially strengthen the faith of many modern believers. Witnessing God at work in the lives of others around them would also encourage the younger generation to have greater faith in Him.

Keep a journal and document your successes regularly if there isn't a venue to share with a group of believers. Additionally, let everyone in your area of influence know about these triumphs. In particular, your family. Remember the little things!

People need positive news from trustworthy individuals since there is so much negative news that they worry about everything from their wealth to their health. Through their expanded lives, the believer should always have a response for others who have not yet accepted their faith!

Let's celebrate and brag about Jesus! Amen!
Visit https://www.BishopLarryJackson.com for a copy of the Faith Infusion journal.

Notes:

_____

_____

_____

_____

_____

_____

_____

_____

_____

_____

_____

_____

_____

_____

DAY 26

Peter's Witness Of Faith In The Gentiles

Acts 15:7-9 And when there had been much disputing, Peter rose up, and said unto them, Men and brethren, ye know how that a good while ago God made choice among us, that the Gentiles by my mouth should hear the word of the gospel, and believe.

And God, which knoweth the hearts, bare them witness, giving them the Holy Ghost, even as he did unto us; And put no difference between us and them, purifying their hearts by faith.

Recall that Jesus instructed the Apostles to travel to the ends of the world, Judea, Jerusalem, and Samaria. Beyond Judea, they disregarded those directives and established their ministry where they were without considering reaching out to others.

But God wasn't going to let them off the hook that easily. So, while Peter rests on top of a roof, he has a dream about unclean animals and is told to eat them. Peter refuses to eat them as anyone in the Jewish tradition would.

God used this opportunity to instruct Peter that nothing called clean can be considered unclean. This would include the Gentiles who had no prior relationship with God. Peter was instructed to follow two men who were sent from Cornelius's house, who was a Gentile, back to his house.

Peter went with the men and preached the gospel of the kingdom to Cornelius' entire family and many of his friends.

When the Holy Ghost filled the house, the Gentile household started speaking in tongues, in the same way the 120 did in the upper room. God's favor on the people was demonstrated even before water baptism was practiced!

The Jerusalem Council discussed whether the Gentiles should be allowed to join the Ekklesia and what rules they needed to abide by. According to Peter, their unadulterated faith allowed God to see them all.

Cornelius' faith put him in the heart of God's desire, and the Father is pleased by faith and will always react to it! That's what our faith will do! Trust your Father; He is waiting for you to move.

Notes:

_____

_____

_____

_____

_____

_____

_____

_____

_____

_____

_____

_____

_____

_____

DAY 27

The Just Live By Faith

The Word 'Faith' is used the Most in Romans 39 times

Romans 1:17 For therein is the righteousness of God revealed from faith to faith: as it is written, The just shall live by faith.

The Apostle Paul returns to Habakkuk to identify how the virtuous should live. The book of Habakkuk, chapter two, verse four, shows a minor variation. Behold, his raised soul is not upright in him (Habakkuk 2:4), but the righteous will live by his faith.

According to Habakkuk, they just follow His (God's) faith.

This phrase appears three times in the New Testament, each with a distinct purpose to draw the reader's attention. First, Paul explains to the Ekklesia in Romans that when believers act in faith, God's righteousness is revealed. Who is willing to advance to higher degrees of faith rather than remain at one level?

Jesus mentioned birds that don't work or store in barns, and we now know some birds consume their body weight daily. The birds rely on God to provide for all of their daily needs. There is never a shortage of supplies or a day lost for the birds! Why would the believer's experience be any different? Our entire existence can—and ought to—be based on trust, for Father God, through Christ Jesus, will supply everything!

Adopt the attitude that I will rely on God no matter what happens or is required! By the way, faith is given to work in the face of life's challenges. Make use of what God has provided! His hand is moved, and His heart is pleased when we trust Him!

Notes:

_____

_____

_____

_____

_____

_____

_____

_____

_____

_____

_____

_____

_____

DAY 28

Faith Established the Law

Romans 3:3 For what if some did not believe? shall their unbelief make the faith of God without effect?

Romans 3:22 Even the righteousness of God which is by faith of Jesus Christ unto all and upon all them that believe: for there is no difference:

Romans 3:25 Whom God hath set forth to be a propitiation through faith in his blood, to declare his righteousness for the remission of sins that are past, through the forbearance of God;

Romans 3:27 Where is boasting then? It is excluded. By what law? of works? Nay: but by the law of faith.

Romans 3:28 Therefore we conclude that a man is justified by faith without the deeds of the law.

Romans 3:30 Seeing it is one God, which shall justify the circumcision by faith, and uncircumcision through faith.

Romans 3:31 Do we then make void the law through faith? God forbid: yea, we establish the law.

The third chapter of Romans is a compelling passage explaining the importance of faith. In his epistle to the Romans, Paul contrasts the distinctions between faith and the law. God's faithfulness cannot be questioned; it takes dedication to accept Jesus' sacrifice. Faith is vastly superior to the law and everything that it requires!

Furthermore, religion helps believers comprehend the law and its requirements! By faith, believers can penetrate inaccessible areas through hard work and legal requirements.

The Ekklesia must now function in kingdom-level faith to demonstrate that Jesus Christ, the Son of God, has come to earth. What do you think was the most recent instance of Father showing up in your life? How did you feel when it happened? To whom did you report the incident?

Everything God is doing through His children should be known to the world. The world cannot deny the body of Christ when it sees the manifestation of God's hand working on our side!

Request additional chances for Father to demonstrate His magnificence to this generation. Keep in mind that the Just Live by Faith!

Notes:

_____

_____

_____

_____

_____

_____

_____

_____

_____

_____

_____

_____

_____

_____

DAY 29

Faith Opens Your Life For Righteousness

Romans 4:5 But to him that worketh not, but believeth on him that justifieth the ungodly, his faith is counted for righteousness.
Romans 4:9 Cometh this blessedness then upon the circumcision only, or upon the uncircumcision also? For we say that faith was reckoned to Abraham for righteousness.

You are not in faith if you try to prove yourself to Father God! Giving money, fasting, reading the Bible, and praying can all be considered acts if they are done to please God. He already loves His children more than they can ever know, and love is the foundation of faith! These actions, above all, react to His love and our trust in Him!

According to Paul, righteousness is deposited into their account when believers trust God. Similarly, God regarded Abraham as righteous since he left his nation without knowing where to go, trusted God to provide him a son in his later years, and was prepared to offer that son as a sacrifice to God.

According to the Bible, human righteousness is nothing more than filthy rags and cannot be compared to God's righteousness! Isaiah 64:6

We all fade like leaves, and our sins have carried us away like the wind. However, we are all like an unclean thing, and our righteousness is like dirty rags.

Being righteous is having the correct standing with God, which calls for faith rather than performance.

Hebrews 11:6 states that it is impossible to please God without faith because a person who approaches him must have trust that he exists and that those who seek him out assiduously will be rewarded.

According to Paul, the Jewish and Gentile believers must approach the Father through Jesus similarly. That way is by and through faith!

Thus, take this test, sit in silence, consider a place where you need God to work, and then see what happens in your heart and mind. Does your mind and heart feel excited, or does worry take center stage? If you were worried, ask the Holy Spirit to strengthen your faith in this area to satisfy your Father.

Ask the Holy Spirit to give you greater faith so you can make even more substantial moves to help you please Father more whenever enthusiasm starts to build. Do not forget that the Just Live by Faith!

Notes:

_____

_____

_____

_____

_____

_____

_____

_____

_____

_____

_____

_____

_____

_____

DAY 30

The Seal of Righteousness

Romans 4:11-12; And he received the sign of circumcision, a seal of the righteousness of the faith which he had yet being uncircumcised: that he might be the father of all them that believe, though they be not circumcised; that righteousness might be imputed unto them also. And the father of circumcision to them who are not of the circumcision only, but who also walk in the steps of that faith of our father Abraham, which he had being yet uncircumcised.

Romans 4:16 Therefore it is of faith, that it might be by grace; to the end the promise might be sure to all the seed; not to that only which is of the law, but to that also which is of the faith of Abraham; who is the father of us all.

Abraham and his seed were promised the right to inherit the world by the righteousness of faith, not the law. Because faith is nullified and the promise made has no effect if those who are of the law become heirs.

Paul ensures that a follower of Christ is fully aware that doing good deeds to win God's favor or attention will not result in righteousness. It is sufficient for a believer to have confidence in God via His Son, Jesus Christ.

The Jewish authorities, who stood for the law and all it required of the people, were very troubled by this thinking. Paul, a former member of the Pharisees, is now advising Gentiles that they are welcome in God's presence and are not required to observe the law.

Paul utilizes Abraham's bond with God before circumcision to support his claim. As stated in Day 29, Abraham's actions react to God and His love for humanity. Abraham was to be circumcised in the body as a result of his obedience and responsiveness to God.

Abraham had a relationship with God and was accepted by him in both circumstances— circumcised and uncircumcised! His children are therefore circumcised "Jews" and uncircumcised "Gentiles."

Once more, faith is the path to righteousness since God bestows it on believers. Recall that when Abraham prayed for Sodom and Gomorrah, he asked if the Angel of the Lord would annihilate the righteous along with the sinful. Through his pleading, he learned that there were not ten righteous in the city!

Additionally, we need to stop believing in ourselves and start believing in God, who alone has the power to make us virtuous. According to the Bible, a believer is God's righteous representative in Christ Jesus. To make us the righteousness of God in him, he made him sin for us, even though he was sinless, according to 2 Corinthians 5:21.

This salvation happened because we believed God for our salvation; now believe Him for your advancement! Remember, The Just Live By Faith!

Notes:

_____

_____

_____

_____

_____

_____

_____

_____

_____

_____

_____

_____

_____

_____

DAY 31

New Hope

Romans 4:18 Who against hope believed in hope, that he might become the father of many nations, according to that which was spoken, So shall thy seed be.

Romans 4:19 And being not weak in faith, he considered not his own body now dead, when he was about an hundred years old, neither yet the deadness of Sara's womb:

Romans 4:20 He staggered not at the promise of God through unbelief; but was strong in faith, giving glory to God;

What a fantastic story! It shows two people who are past their prime, childbearing, and child-producing years and are told by God that they will become parents. These two people wanted to produce a child throughout their marriage, but circumstances kept this from happening for no fault of their own.

They are now given a promise from the Lord that gives them hope! Abraham believed in hope, which is why the remark against it is so powerful: Sometimes, the old hope might prevent the new hope from being received.

Personally, I think it's great that Paul says Abraham had strong faith, which was demonstrated by the fact that he didn't take into account his advanced age. Nor his body's inability to bear children, or Sarah's incapacity to conceive. She is now an elderly woman in addition to being unable to conceive!

When I was younger, I observed both men and women who drank alcohol stumbling around until they were unable to get up and falling to the ground. Stumbling typically indicates a problem with one's standing capacity and maintaining balance.

According to Paul, unbelief is more powerful than 1000-proof alcohol because, while alcohol wears off, unbelief lingers in one's life unnoticed, allowing someone to continue drinking for years. When the Lord spoke to Abraham, he didn't drink from the bottle of unbelief and only considered what the Lord said.

We frequently sit through services when the Lord teaches us, or we read the Bible on our own, and the Lord reveals things to us. But we can take a small sip of doubt and let other things from our past cloud the revelation.

The very thing that the Lord desires for our lives disappears before we can ever experience it because we are intoxicated before realizing it!

It's time to stop drinking and have faith!

Notes:

_____

_____

_____

_____

_____

_____

_____

_____

_____

_____

_____

_____

_____

Made in the USA
Columbia, SC
27 February 2025

54466832R10059